To:

_____

FINNEY COUNTY PUBLIC LIBRARY
605 E WALNUT ST
GARDEN CITY KS 67846

From:

_____

Date:

_____

D1243490

What Will HEAVEN Be Like?

By Kathleen Ruckman

Illustrated by Greg Hardin and Robert Vann

HARVEST HOUSE PUBLISHERS

EUGENE, OREGON

What Will **HEAVEN** Be Like?

Text Copyright © 2010 by Kathleen Ruckman
Artwork Copyright © 2010 by Greg Hardin and Robert Vann

Published by Harvest House Publishers
Eugene, Oregon 97402
www.harvesthousepublishers.com

ISBN 978-0-7369-2571-6

Original illustrations by Greg Hardin

Design and production by Mary pat Design, Westport, Connecticut

Printed in China

10 11 12 13 14 15 16 / LP / 10 9 8 7 6 5 4 3 2 1

With special thoughts of my brother and his wife, Gary and Laynie,
my nephew and niece, Adam and Angela, and our family—in
remembrance of Aaron, who lives on in our hearts.

There will be a Grand Reunion in heaven some day,
and it will be more wonderful than we can imagine!
—Kathleen Ruckman

Soli Deo Gloria

★ ★ ★

For my nephews Andrew, Colton, and the unnamed baby on the way.
—Greg Hardin

For Caitlyn and Marina, and remembering Cullen.
—Robert Vann

Annie and Adam are sister and brother. Every Sunday afternoon they visit Grandpa's farm in the country. Annie and Adam give Grandpa a big hug when they go to visit.

Rows of corn and wheat blow in the wind on Grandpa's land. The tall cornstalks look as if they're waving at Annie and Adam, and the wheat gleams like gold in the sun. Out in the field, a bright red silo reaches to the sky. Grandpa's farm is a fun place to visit and stay all day!

Annie and Adam love to take walks with Grandpa and see the lambs, cows, and pigs. Grandpa takes their hands, and off they go. Grandpa's dog, Stanley, wags his tail and tags along. The barn kittens arch their backs and cry, "meow!" as Stanley scampers by.

Most of all, Annie loves the wildflowers that grow along the country road. She bends down and picks sweet buttercups and purple violets as Stanley barks at the butterflies! He's a silly, playful dog, and going for walks with him is fun!

They hear the whack of a hammer and the buzz of a power saw nearby. Workers are building a new house across the field.

"Jesus is building us a home in heaven!" says Annie. "My Sunday school teacher says so."

"And the Bible says so too," Grandpa tells the children. "Jesus said His house is like a mansion with many rooms and that we'll live in a wonderful city. He's working on it all right now!"

Bessie the cow moos a friendly "Good afternoon" as her little calf pokes its head through the fence and looks up at Annie with big brown eyes.

"What will heaven be like, Grandpa?" asks Annie, who is just getting over a bad cold. She sneezes so loud that Bessie's ears perk up!

"Heaven is a lot of things," Grandpa says, as he throws a stick for Stanley to fetch. "First, it's a place where no one ever gets sick."

"You mean I'd *never* catch a cold or have an earache in heaven?" asks Annie, as she picks a bright yellow daffodil.

"That's right," says Grandpa, "no sickness and no pain."

"I'll bet no one is sad in heaven either," says Annie.

"Right again! The Bible says that heaven is such a bright and happy place that we won't even need the sun!" says Grandpa. "And God will wipe away all of our tears."

"The way *you* do, Grandpa!" Annie says, twirling round and round. "Oh, I'm sooooo dizzy!" she squeals.

"Come with me, Grandpa!" Annie says, as she pulls Grandpa by the hand into the meadow. "Look at all the daisies. Look at all the dandelions—and the teeny-tiny blue flowers hiding in the grass!"

"I'd have to bend *way* down to see those tiny ones, Annie, and these old knees won't let me."

"Don't worry, Grandpa. I'll pick them and show you!" Annie says, as she plucks a few tiny blooms and adds them to her bouquet.

11

"Here comes a snowstorm!" Adam shouts as he runs to Annie, tightly gripping a bunch of dandelions with fluffy white seeds that blow away like snowflakes in the wind.

"Look at the pansies!" Annie tells Adam, pointing to the colorful patch. "They look like little faces smiling up at us!" And she bends down to carefully add more blossoms to her bundle.

13

A boy rides by on his bicycle. After making a face and sticking out his tongue at Adam, he pedals on down the country road.

"He's always mean when I come to visit," says Adam. "Will people be mean in heaven?"

"The Bible says that God is love, and when we're with God in heaven, we'll love each other the way He loves," says Grandpa. "You can show God's love to this boy by being kind."

"Are you saying I shouldn't make a face back at him?" asks Adam.

"That's right," says Grandpa. "God is love, and He wants His ways done on earth as they are done in heaven. God wants us to love one another even when someone is mean."

Grandpa's blue eyes twinkle when he talks about God's love.

"In Sunday school, we learned that we should love one another," Adam says as Stanley chases the boy on his bike, barking all the way down the dusty road.

The children and Grandpa come to a pond. "Hey! I see frogs in there!" says Adam. "If I catch that frog, can I take it home?"

"You can—*if* you can catch it!" Grandpa says with a grin.

Adam *almost* makes the catch, but the frog leaps right out of his hands. Muddy from following the croaking sound, Adam suddenly stops and notices the dragonflies dancing in the air above his head. "Look!" he shouts out to Annie and Grandpa. "These bugs look like tiny helicopters!" They all giggle as one shiny blue dragonfly almost lands on Adam's nose.

"Pick some cattails for me!" Annie calls to Adam.

Adam sloshes to the edge of the pond and tugs on a cattail. "Whoa!" he shouts, losing his balance and falling backward into the soft, squishy grass.

Sheep are grazing in a field nearby. "Baaaaa," they call out, making a sweet but shaky sound. The three wander over to the fence to see the newborn lambs. "I love the baby lambs, Grandpa," says Annie.

Noticing a prickly wild rose growing on the fence, Annie *very* carefully picks it and asks, "Grandpa, who will be in heaven?"

"Everyone who knows and loves Jesus," says Grandpa. "The Bible says that if we're born again—that means if Jesus lives in our hearts—then we will see heaven."

Grandpa puts his arms around the children. "We are like those sheep," he says. "The Bible says that God is our shepherd. He guides us and takes good care of us. When we die and go to heaven, we won't be scared because God our shepherd will go with us. He'll walk right beside us, and we'll live forever in heaven!"

Grandpa and the children stop at the pen where the baby pigs are squealing. Grandpa tosses dried corn on the cob to the mother pig.

"I'm getting hungry too," says Adam, as he chews on a stalk of wheat. "Grandpa, will people eat in heaven?"

Grandpa stops for a minute to think. His forehead always gets wrinkly when he thinks.

"The Bible says that Jesus will make a wonderful supper party in heaven," Grandpa says. "It won't be the kind of food we eat here, but we'll have a great celebration because we'll be with Jesus forever and ever!"

"A party? Let's get packin' for heaven!" says Annie, as she tosses some corn over the fence.

They hear a horse trotting nearby and look up to see Annie's friend Sarah waving a friendly hello. Sarah will soon move to another town.

"Grandpa, I wish Sarah didn't have to leave," says Annie sadly. "I'll miss playing with her when I come to visit you."

"Sometimes those we love have to go away," says Grandpa, "but Jesus is our best friend who is *always* with us—now and forever in heaven too. The Bible says so."

"I'm glad Jesus is my *very* best friend," Annie says, as she picks some bright orange poppies. "Jesus won't ever move away because He lives in my heart!"

"Grandpa, what are you whistling?" asks Annie.

"It's an old song we used to sing at church," Grandpa says tenderly. "It was one of Grandma's favorites. It's called, 'When We All Get to Heaven.'"

"Oh," Annie says and then tries her best to whistle along with Grandpa. Giving up she says, "No one can whistle like *you* do, Grandpa!"

Noticing Adam's bulging pockets, Grandpa says with a chuckle, "You sure are carrying a lot of cargo, and it looks like more than just pebbles and rocks."

"I have—a frog!" Adam shouts, pulling the little critter out, startling his sister, and making Stanley bark. Popping out of Adam's hands, the slippery frog disappears into Grandpa's garden.

Grandpa's front porch has a swing where Grandma and Grandpa used to sit together. Annie sadly looks at the swing and then places a flower on the seat.

"I'm sure glad there's a forever," Annie says, looking up at Grandpa.

"Me too," he says with the same twinkle he had in his eyes as when he sat there with Grandma.

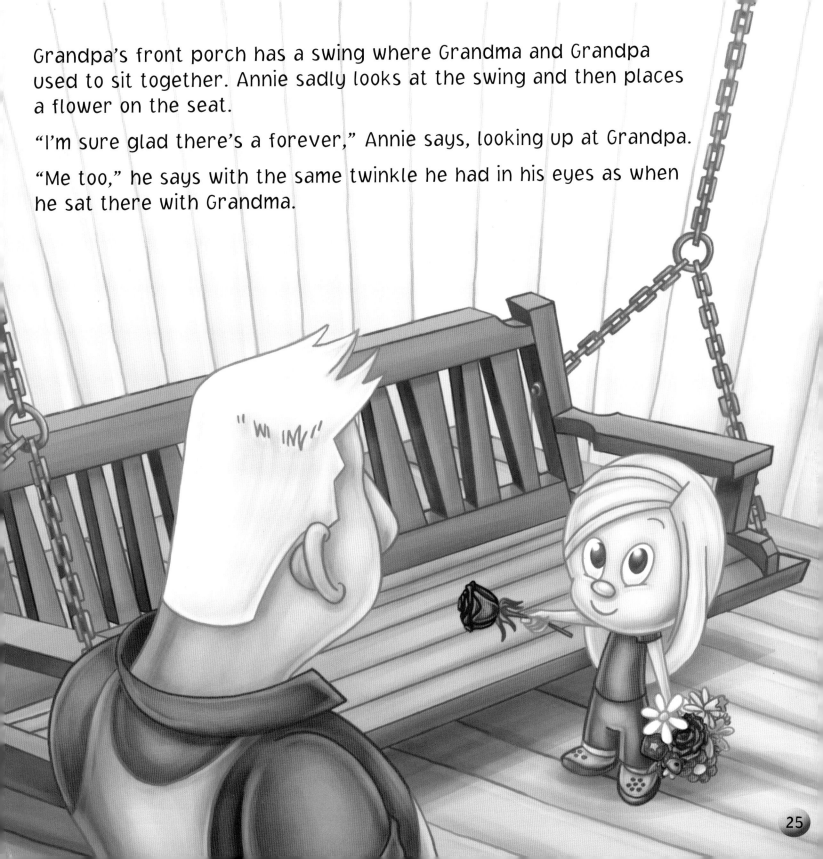

The screen door slams as Grandpa, Annie, and Adam walk into the kitchen. Stanley tags behind, and his tail *almost* gets caught in the door!

"I picked lots and lots of flowers, Grandpa! Aren't they beautiful?" Annie says beaming.

"So many colors, and they smell nice too—like perfume!"

"Grandma used to say, 'Didn't the Lord think of everything!'" Grandpa reminds the children, as they talk about the flowers God created.

"My flowers need a drink!" says Annie, as she stands on tiptoes to get a vase. She puts her colorful bouquet in the vase, adds water from the faucet, and places it on Grandpa's table.

Adam dunks a cookie in a glass of ice cold milk. "Look at my milk mustache!" he says with an extra-wide, mischievous grin.

"You are so funny!" Annie giggles and then hops onto her chair, as Stanley begs for a cookie from under the table.

Annie says, "I wish my flowers wouldn't die, but they always do. Grandpa, do you think heaven is a place where flowers live forever?"

"And do you think we'll have a pet like Stanley in heaven?" interrupts Adam, as he sneaks a piece of cookie for Stanley.

Grandpa thinks again. His forehead wrinkles.

"We'll just have to wait and see," he says, "because the Bible doesn't tell us about flowers or puppies. But I suspect that whatever is beautiful and whatever makes us happy just might be there. We'll have to wait and see. God has been planning heaven for a *very* long time—and it will be more wonderful than we can imagine!"

Soon it was time to leave. "I'll miss you, Grandpa. I don't want to say goodbye!" Annie says with a frown.

"In heaven there will be no more goodbyes—only hellos!" Grandpa says with a smile.

"You mean like saying hello to Grandma in heaven someday?" asks Adam.

"Yes," Grandpa says, "like saying hello on a bright and happy morning!"

"See you next week, Grandpa!" the children say, as Mother and Father pick them up at the farm. "We can't wait to find out what we talk about *next* Sunday!"

31

Parent/Teacher Guide

Open a Bible and show the children the following verses describing heaven (NKJV). Read the Scriptures out loud together and explain that the Bible is God's special love letter to them—to be read now and as they grow up.

- God is building us a home in heaven—John 14:2

- There will be no pain or sorrow in heaven; a bright and happy place—Revelation 21:4; 22:5

- God is love—1 John 4:8

- Love others as God has loved you—John 15:12

- God wants His ways done on earth as they are done in heaven—Matthew 6:9-10

- Those who are born again will be in heaven because they know and love Jesus—John 3:3

- When we die, God walks with us so we won't be scared, and in heaven, we will never die—Psalm 23:4,6

- There will be a great celebration supper in heaven—Revelation 19:9

- Jesus is our very best friend now and forever and will never leave us—Proverbs 18:24; Hebrews 13:5

- Heaven will be more wonderful than we can ever imagine—1 Corinthians 2:9